GOYA

An artist for an age   4

Youth, training, early works   4

Goya at the Madrid Court (1774-1792)   6
    The tapestry cartoons   6
    Goya joins the Academy   8

Illness, disillusionment and enlightenment
(1792-1807)   12

The War of Independence and the absolutist
period (1808-1824)   22
    A time of war   22
    A disappointing peace   22
    The black paintings   28

Exile in France (1824-1828)   30

AN ARTIST FOR AN AGE

The true testimony of the artistic genius of Francisco de Goya (1746-1828) is his painting, as he is one of the best represented artists at the Museo del Prado. Goya was both a man of his time and a universal artist. He was painter to the Spanish court but also a friend of the few Spaniards who welcomed the Enlightenment, sharing with them the same sense of justice and distaste for religious fanaticism and superstition. However, his vision of an incoherent world inhabited by things ignoble, culminating in the spine-chilling engravings of *The Disasters of War*, shows just how far Goya distanced himself from the idealistic faith in the power of reason and the progress of man which his enlightened counterparts professed. A contemporary in the strictest sense of the French artist Jacques-Louis David (1748-1825), who became the painter of the French Revolution, Goya went beyond the ideals of fatherland and honour which the latter extolled, reflecting the absurdity of heroism, the pointlessness of any martyrdom and the horror of human wartime atrocities in paintings such as *The Third of May: The Mass Execution at Príncipe Pío* affording victors and vanquished the same dramatic force. He reproaches reason for its impotence and denounces the uncontrollable violence of the illogic and madness that incessantly assail the human mind.

YOUTH, TRAINING, EARLY WORKS

Goya was born in 1746 in Fuendetodos, a small Aragonese town near Saragossa.

At fourteen he joined the workshop of Saragossan painter José Luzán (1710-1785), a friend of the family. He soon felt the need to measure his strength in the capital, where he would have better chances of developing a career. He applied to join the Academy of Fine Arts in 1763 and 1764, but failed to gain any recognition for his works.

In 1770 he set out on a voyage to Italy which was to last almost a year. During this time he lived in Rome and Parma, where he took part in a contest organised by the city's Academy with his work *Hannibal the Conqueror Contemplates Italy for the first time from the Alps* (Fundación Selgas Falgade, Cudillero, Asturias).

By the end of 1771 he was back in Saragossa, painting *Adoration of the Name of God* on the cupola of the choir in the cathedral of Nuestra Señora del Pilar. Although markedly baroque, this work nonetheless represents a shift away from painstaking detail and a greater use of rapid brushstrokes and particular concern for the light effects.

In 1773 Goya married Josefa Bayeu, the sister of the deputy director of the San Fernando Academy of Fine Arts and court painter, Francisco Bayeu. It may have been a marriage of convenience, though marriages between members of the same profession were very common. Goya's first *Self-Portrait* (private collection) dates from those years. However, his most important accomplishment during that period was the eleven oil paintings over three metres high for the Carthusian monastery of Aula Dei near Saragossa, of which only seven survive and are in a bad state of preservation. They

Josefa Bayeu (?). *Museo del Prado*.

GOYA

EDICIONES
Aldeasa

depict scenes from the life of the Virgin Mary, which the painter placed in an architectural setting done in simple, emphatically drawn lines to enhance their monumentality and theatricality.

GOYA AT THE MADRID COURT (1774-1792)

The tapestry cartoons

Goya moved to Madrid at the end of 1774 at the request of the German painter Anton Raphaël Mengs (1728-1779) to work at the Royal Tapestry Factory of Santa Bárbara, of which Mengs was director at the time. The Royal Factories had been established under the reign of Philip V and sprang from the need to stop money flowing out of the country on account of imports of luxury items. During the reign of Charles III, the Royal Factory of Santa Bárbara enjoyed a period of glory under the direction of Mengs, who engaged many young artists to work on the so-called "cartoons", which were in fact oil paintings on canvas that were used as models by the tapestry weavers. Almost all these cartoons now hang in the Prado.

Tapestry cartoons were one of Goya's first commissions from the court, and he was engaged in these efforts for nearly twenty years (1773-1791). The cartoons depicted Flemish genre scenes in the manner of Teniers or Wouwerman, or Italian scenes in the manner of Corrado Giaquinto. Goya broke with this tradition, turning to popular Madrid themes depicting types and customs associated with life in Spain, with an increasingly rich palette enhanced with light effects.

His first series comprising nine cartoons was intended to decorate the Princes' dining room at El Escorial. For this summer residence, which was also used as a hunting lodge, he was commissioned to paint hunting themes, such as *The Hunter and His Dogs*. This cartoon clearly displays Goya's talent for portraying animals and his masterful evocation of the complicity between the hunter and his hounds. The vegetation adapts to the setting without creating tension.

The second series, consisting of ten cartoons (1776-1778), was for the dining room of the Princes of Asturias at El Pardo. After completing *The Picnic* Goya commented proudly that it was "de ynbención mía" (my invention). Painstaking attention is paid to the details of each of the human figures. One of the most famous works in this series, *The Parasol*, fully conveys the "jocular" aspect of Madrid life, both in the extreme freshness and luminosity of the colours, with subtle half-tones in the shaded area beneath the parasol, and in the theme: in the foreground, a young women sitting with a little dog on her lap and a *majo* (dandy) holding a sunshade to protect her from the sun, arranged in pyramidal fashion over the background landscape. This simple composition displays the influence of French rococo painting. For the first time in Goya's painting, the young women gazes flirtatiously and brazenly at the viewer, leading him to believe he is the one she is smiling at.

Between 1778 and 1780 Goya completed twelve cartoons for El Pardo palace. They

Top left, The Angler *(detail).* Right, The Hunter with his Dogs *(detail).*
Bottom, The Parasol. *Museo del Prado.*

were intended for the antechamber and bedchamber of the Princes of Asturias. The first in this series was *The Blind Guitarist*. The blind guitarist was a popular figure who sold romances and informed of recent news, accompanied by his guide. In this scene other people are listening to him: two women, a foreigner and a black water-seller. Goya uses spotlighting to emphasise the most important figures rather than overall illumination, and the composition is again pyramidal, as recommended by Mengs. Other cartoons in this series are *Fair at Madrid* and *The Crockery Vendor*.

This shift towards Spanish everyday reality, linked to the development of the ideas of the Enlightenment, indicates that a revolution was taking place in painting, though not in the main genres but in one that was regarded almost as secondary, was perhaps supervised less closely by the Academy, and in which painting therefore enjoyed greater freedom.

Between 1786 and 1788 Goya completed a further series for the dining room of the Princes of Asturias at El Pardo. In these paintings he highlighted in a non-euphemistic manner the social and economic gap between two opposite worlds, as can be seen in *The Wounded Mason, Poor People by a Fountain* and *The Snowstorm or Winter* (Museo del Prado). The latter painting, the composition of which is reminiscent of the genre of historical pictures created by Jean-Antoine Gros, nonetheless differs from the work of the French artist in that it conveys greater emotion through the bleak and dismal landscape in which the people – soldiers or peasants – appear to be doomed to a certain

death, the dog shows its fear with its tail between its legs, and the only glimmer of hope is symbolised by the little bird the central figure is holding.

The series of cartoons for the Infantas' bedchamber at El Pardo (1788-1789) was unfinished when Charles III died. The few cartoons from this series include the painting of the popular game known as *Blind Man's Buff*.

It appears that Goya became less and less interested in continuing to paint tapestry cartoons. There are testimonies of complaints sent by the director of the Factory to the new king about the attitude of Goya, who "neither paints nor is willing to paint". However, he did a last series for Charles IV's office at El Escorial (1791-1792) with carnivalesque amusements such as *The Straw Manikin* as their main theme. Four women holding a blanket toss a young man into the air as if he were a puppet – an ironic metaphor of women's sway over men, and a symbol of their sexual appetite. The composition is again simple and pyramidal and the figures stand out more prominently against the space in which they are immersed, creating their own volume by means of the effects of light.

Goya joins the Academy

While engaged by the tapestry factory, Goya produced other works, such as the *Christ on the Cross* (Museo del Prado, 1780) which secured him admission – by unanimous decision – to the San Fernando Academy of Fine Arts. Three fundamental aspects influenced the decision of the academy members. First, the orthodox

Christ on the Cross. *Museo del Prado.*

iconographic treatment of the theme: Christ with four nails, as Pacheco advocated in his *Treatise*, and the inscription in Hebrew, Greek and Latin on a small panel atop a pedestal. Second, the pictorial references to Mengs and Velázquez, the most highly esteemed painters of the time. Goya's Christ, who displays no signs of suffering, has the same beauty as the *Crucifixion of Christ* by Mengs at Aranjuez and is depicted at the same moment, before death; from Velázquez he borrowed the idea of focusing on the figure, eliminating the background landscape, in order to convey a sense of timelessness. A third factor was the choice of genre, an "academia", that is a nude, one of the main exercises performed by students of fine arts. There has been much discussion about the devotional meaning of Goya's religious works. In this case, his intention was obviously not religious.

By this time Goya had built up an aristocratic clientele. In 1782 the Count of Floridablanca entrusted him with one of the paintings that were to decorate the church of San Francisco el Grande, *The Sermon of St Bernardino of Sienna*. In August 1783 the Infante Don Luis de Borbón invited Goya to his palace in Arenas de San Pedro, where he painted portraits of the Infante's family, including *The Family of the Infante Don Luis* (1783) a highly remarkable group portrait which conveys the atmosphere of intimacy in which Don Luis lived, far from the etiquette of the court.

On 1 May 1785 Goya was made deputy director of painting at the Academy, and a year later was appointed painter to the king. Shortly afterwards, putting behind him the earlier squabbles with his brother-in-law over artistic matters, he painted a portrait of *Francisco Bayeu*, probably as a token of gratitude for Bayeu's support in securing these appointments.

ILLNESS, DISILLUSIONMENT AND ENLIGHTENMENT (1792-1807)

At the end of 1792 Goya travelled around Andalusia. In Seville he was stricken with a serious illness that forced him to return to Cadiz, where he spent six months at the home of his friend Sebastián Martínez, whose portrait he had recently completed, until he recovered. This illness was to leave him deaf.

He returned to Madrid in 1793 and painted the *Self-Portrait* which hangs in the Academy of Fine Arts. Goya portrayed himself against the light, by a tall window in which his silhouette stands out, facing a big easel with paintbrushes. Perhaps he is questioning his own ability to continue with his activity, though this portrait could also be interpreted as a fresh affirmation of his painting.

Goya made a second trip to Andalusia in 1796. This time he painted three frescoes for the oratory of the Santa Cueva in Cadiz : *Miracle of the Loaves and Fishes*, *The Parable of the Wedding Guest* and *The Last Supper*. All three are related to the sacrament of the Eucharist, a theme of primary importance to the brotherhood of the Santa Cueva. A noteworthy feature of these paintings is the successive planes in depth, the varying foreshortening and their dramatic expressiveness. That same year Goya was invited to the palace of the Duke

The Duchess of Alba and her Duenna. Page 10, The Wounded Mason. Page 11, The Straw Manikin. Museo del Prado.

and Duchess of Alba in Sanlúcar de Barrameda. The duke died that year and Cayetana, the duchess, stayed in Sanlúcar with Goya for three months. What occurred between the painter and the duchess during those months is not known. In a letter to his friend Martín Zapater, Goya tells of his interest in her, which is borne out by the drawings in the sketchbook known as the *Cuaderno de Sanlúcar* of which Cayetana is unquestionably the main subject. Other information indicates that this interest was mutual, such as the fact that around that time the duchess changed her will, leaving a life annuity to Goya's son. Particularly significant is the portrait housed in the Hispanic Society, in which duchess is wearing two rings, one of which bears the inscription "Alba" and the other "Goya", and at her feet is an even more revealing inscription in the sand, "Sólo (only) Goya". This would suggest that Goya, by then in his fifties, must have had a great passion for Cayetana, who was thirty-six. They may have been lovers for a time, though the duchess's capricious nature was soon to put an end to the relationship, bringing Goya back to reality with a bump. It is perhaps this disillusionment that is conveyed in the engraving *Dream of Lies and Inconstancy*, in which the painter embraces a Cayetana with two faces, one of which is turned towards him while the other one has its gaze fixed on another suitor. The butterfly's wings further accentuate the idea of flightiness.

During his sojourn in Cádiz, apart from the episode involving the Duchess of Alba, Goya had the chance to frequent the company of some enlightened intellectuals such as Sebastián Martínez y Moratín, who were to become his closest friends and prompted his change of mentality as to his way of looking at the world, to which he was somewhat predisposed. Around this time he painted the portraits of *Bernardo Iriarte*, *Meléndez Valdés* and *Martín Zapater*.

During the nineties, Goya worked on the series known as the *Caprichos*, including some drawings from a previous series, the so-called *Sketchbook B*, which consisted of thirty seven numbered sheets with drawings on both sides (23.6 x 14.6 cm). It was completed in 1799. It comprises eighty plates (21.8 x 15.5 cm) etched with aquatint, at the time a new technique which afforded him greater expressiveness as it enabled him to achieve more intense contrasts of light and tonality, even obtaining tactile qualities. Each *Capricho* bears a caption that sometimes explains to an extent the meaning of the image. The Prado houses the explanatory autograph manuscript which accompanied the copy he gave the king, in which he sometimes camouflaged or embellished the true meaning of the drawings.

Around 1798 he also painted the portrait of *Gaspar Melchor de Jovellanos* (Museo del Prado), which has a very balanced composition and displays a certain melancholy. On the desk it is possible to make out a statue of Minerva, the goddess of the arts, her outstretched arm symbolising wisdom.

In 1798 Goya painted a set of frescoes for the chapel of San Antonio de la Florida in Madrid, which was built around the time according to neo-classical taste for the Italian architect Filippo Fontana (1744-1800). The one in the apse depicts

Don Gaspar Melchor de Jovellanos. *Museo del Prado.*

The Trinity, while the barrel vaults, pendentives and lunettes flanking the central vault display angels with female forms. For the cupola he did *The Miracle of St Anthony of Padua*, an episode seldom depicted in painting, in which the saint's father is accused of a committing a crime and convicted. St Anthony resuscitates the dead man in order that he may testify to his father's innocence. Two further commissions which can be dated to around 1798 also relate to religious themes. The first was the *The Taking of Christ* for Toledo cathedral, in which Goya strives to place his creation in the context of an earlier pictorial tradition close to El Greco's *The Disrobing of Christ*. Goya comes close to El Greco's manner of composition in an attempt to emulate and even improve on his painting, achieving a dramatic pictorial quality and using markedly contrasting light and shade to intensify the scene.

As first court painter Goya was entrusted with the portraits of *Queen María Luisa*, in a style similar to that found in the *The Marchioness of Santa Cruz* and *Charles IV as Huntsman*. It is known that in 1800 Manuel Godoy, Charles IV's all-powerful prime minister, had portraits of himself and of his wife *The Countess of Chinchón* (Museo del Prado) at his home. This is one of Goya's most famous portraits and unquestionably one of his masterpieces. The sitter, María Teresa de Borbón y Vallabriga, was the daughter of the Infante Don Luis de Borbón, Charles III's brother. Her mother was an Aragonese noblewoman, María Teresa de Vallabriga y Rozas, who did not hail from the same social class as the Infante. This distanced them from the

Madrid court and from contact with the royal family. The future countess was born in Arenas de San Pedro on 6 March 1779. Her father died when she was six years old, causing her and her brother to be sent to the Royal Convent of San Clemente in Toledo. Shortly after she turned eighteen, Charles IV informed her of his decision to marry her to Manuel Godoy. The portrait was painted three years after the marriage, when she was pregnant; the tiara of ears of corn on her head, a symbol of fertility, alludes to this. On her right hand she displays a large ring, probably with a likeness of Godoy. The colours, lights and drawing and the composition, perspective and atmosphere of the painting all form a harmonious whole. The result is a work of high quality which conveys the complicity between painter and sitter. Goya, who had known her since she was a small child, skilfully portrays to the full the delicacy and shyness of the elegant countess in a gesture of delightful abandonment. The viewer notes a calm and assumed feeling of solitude that is heightened by the absence of specific spatial references, which shrouds her in an atmosphere of timelessness.

The commission for *The Naked Maja* (Museo del Prado) and *The Clothed Maja* (Museo del Prado) must have come from Godoy towards 1797, though we cannot be absolutely sure. However, this is the most likely explanation, owing both to the fact that the painting belonged to his collection and to his known taste for female nudes. These nudes, including Velázquez's *The Toilet of Venus*, hung on the walls of his private office. By 1800 he had come to own both paintings, which were queried by the

The Naked Maja and The Clothed Maja. *Museo del Prado.*

Tribunal of the Inquisition on account of their "obscene subject-matter". Goya may have taken Titian's Venus paintings as a point of departure in his composition, but he shifted away from them to create a new category of female nude. The Maja's pose lacks the naivety of the earlier Venuses: she is neither asleep, nor feigning obliviousness, nor looking away unaware she is being observed; rather, she has her arms behind her head and unashamedly exhibits herself. For the first time in the history of painting, pubic hair is shown. She is a flesh-and-blood woman who revels in her sexual appeal, provoking the spectator. The title of "Maja" (denoting showiness) given to her by the Inquisition may spring more from her brazenness than from her costume. The pictures are painted with great ease and powerful colour contrasts that afford them an obvious sensuality. The legend that assumes them to be portraits of the Duchess of Alba is not entirely ungrounded, as although the face of the Majas is clearly not Cayetana's, the body could be, for it is reminiscent of the sketches Goya made around that time in the so-called *Album A*. In the painting of the clothed Maja, the broad ribbon that encircles her body is likewise similar to those found in Goya's portraits of the duchess.

One of the painter's best documented works is *The Family of Charles IV* (Museo del Prado) which he worked on in 1800 in Aranjuez (the sketches) and Madrid (the final version). In a frieze-like arrangement, from left to right, are Don Carlos María Isidro; Goya painting; Ferdinand, Prince of Asturias; Doña María Josefa, Charles IV's sister; an unknown princess with her face turned – this could be the future Princess of Asturias, whose identity was not yet known, or Carlota Joaquina, another daughter of Charles IV and queen of Portugal, who was not in Madrid around this time; Doña María Isabel; Queen María Luisa; Don Francisco de Paula; King Charles IV; Don Antonio Pascual, the king's brother, and on his left the Prince and Princess of Parma, Don Luis de Borbón and his wife Doña María Luisa Josefina, holding their son Carlos Luis. Behind the Prince of Parma is another unknown woman. Once again the question arises of whether this could be Carlota Joaquina or María Amalia, the king's late daughter.

The space portrayed is almost a corridor with two paintings hung on the back wall. Standing by his easel, Goya is painting in semi-darkness. Despite the obvious reference to *The Maids of Honour*, the Goya who is portrayed does not display the same professionalism as Velázquez; rather, he gazes pensively at the viewer. Goya's spatial arrangement is far-removed from any lesson in complicated planes of perspective. He denies any illusion of depth. His painting is more a study of patches of light and shadow, of the contrast of brightness and colour. The portraits show real faces that are neither handsome nor ugly. The queen is in the centre of the canvas. The work thus represents a closed and stifling world, in which breathing space is scarce. This portrait marks the culmination of Goya's official career and he did not paint for the king and queen again until 1808, when he did a portrait of Ferdinand VII.

Also from this period is the 1805 portrait of the *Marchioness of Santa Cruz* (Museo

The Countess of Chinchón. *Museo del Prado.*

del Prado) characterised as Erato, the muse of lyric poetry, dressed in Empire style with soft and brilliant fabrics which have a tactile appearance.

THE WAR OF INDEPENDENCE AND THE ABSOLUTIST PERIOD (1808-1824)

A time of war

The revolt of Aranjuez took place on 17 March 1808. The populace staged an uprising against Godoy, whom Charles IV dismissed, stepping down from the throne in favour of his son Ferdinand VII. Goya had just completed an equestrian portrait of Ferdinand. That same year saw the French intervention. Napoleon met the Spanish royal family at Bayonne and compelled the king to abdicate in favour of Napoleon's brother Joseph Bonaparte.

Goya remained in Madrid and continued to paint for the new king, Joseph I, who commissioned him to do an *Allegory of the City of Madrid* featuring the image of the sovereign on one side. The fluctuating political situation caused this likeness to be subsequently replaced by the word "Constitution", which was again painted over and eventually replaced with a portrait of the new king Ferdinand VII. It was not Goya but the members of his workshop who made these alterations.

Around 1808 Goya painted a major set of twelve still lifes. The *Dead Turkey* at the Prado (Museo del Prado) is one of them. Goya's still lifes display no spatial co-ordinates to guide us: the turkey could be on the ground or flying with outstretched wings. This ambiguous manner of viewing his subject matter is an important innovation. Also worthy of mention is the instinctive feeling he provokes in the viewer by portraying the defenceless animal as a victim, lying in a pitiful state on top of the wicker basket, a device Goya uses to move us. These animal paintings are extremely modern, close to Courbet's or Manet's still lifes.

In 1810 he must have begun to think about the series of prints of the *Disasters of War*. The new technique of etching enabled him to create powerful contrasts of light and shade that heighten the visual impact of these scenes, which are intended to provoke horror and emotion.

Goya's wife, Josefa Bayeu, died in 1812. Around this time he painted *Sketchbook E*, comprising fifty numbered wash drawings in Chinese ink, of which only forty survive. These have black edges and are larger than the previous ones (27 x 19 cm). As is usually the case with Goya, each bears a title. These drawings generally depict two figures which convey the artist's harsh criticism of social vices, with a simple technique and marked chiaroscuro that accentuate their expressiveness.

A disappointing peace

The French troops finally withdrew from Spain in 1814 and Ferdinand VII returned to Madrid. Goya approached the regent, Cardinal Luis de Borbón, offering "to perpetuate through my paintbrush the most noteworthy and heroic actions and scenes of our glorious insurrection against the tyrant of Europe". This led to the

Top, Dead Turkey. *Bottom,* The Second of May 1808: the Charge of the Mamelukes. *Previous double page,* The Family of Charles IV. *Museo del Prado.*

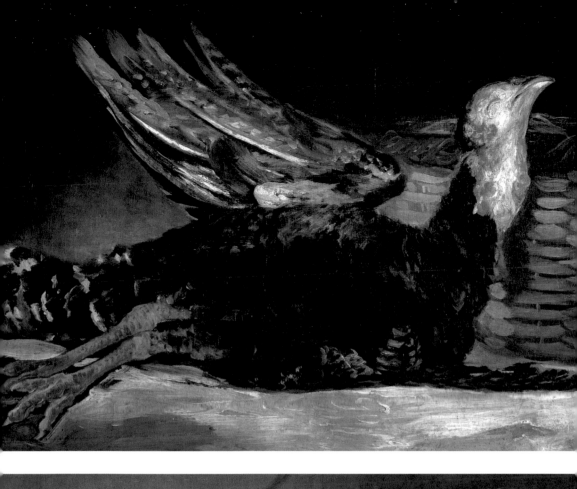

paintings depicting the events of 2 and 3 May 1808. *The Third of May 1808: The Mass Execution at Príncipe Pío* (Museo del Prado) shows, on the right, a group of soldiers lined up and ready to shoot at a friar and five villagers who await the gunfire on the left. Three corpses lie on the ground and there is a group of condemned men in the background. The buildings of Madrid can be made out in the darkness of the distant background. Historian Hugh Honour suggests that Goya modelled his painting on Antoine-Jean Gros's renderings of "historic events" such as *Napoleon Visiting the Pesthouse at Jaffa* (1804). Gros, whose works were widely disseminated in Europe during that period thanks to printing, became a benchmark for his generation of painters, advocating a new, more realistic model that supplanted Jacques-Louis David's idealism. In Goya's work, the dramatic intensity is focused on the man in the white shirt who is kneeling before the faceless firing squad with his arms up in the air. This work, supposedly intended to suggest that the men shot in 1808 did not die in vain, nonetheless arouses in viewers a broader and deeper feeling. Goya did not choose any well-known hero but rather a shabby villager, a poor man whom the French troops in Madrid stumbled across and who is going to die as a martyr. The other person who has been killed and is lying at his feet accentuates the absurdity of this sacrifice. Both are faceless beings because they could be anyone. The only source of light is the soldiers' large square lantern. Everything seems to have failed. The individual artist is the only person who is able to find meaning in a

chaotic world. Goya's vision is too embittered and violent to distract the viewer's attention from the horror of the subject depicted.

In 1815 he did two self-portraits, one on panel, which hangs in the San Fernando Academy of Fine Arts, and another on canvas, which is housed in the Prado (Museo del Prado). In these paintings the artist portrays himself unpretentiously, without showing us his social status, trade, tastes or important clients. The self-portrait in the Academy is signed and dated. The one at the Prado differs somewhat as to the position of the head, the collar of the shirt and, in particular, the facial expression, which denotes greater vivacity. It is known that during those years Goya again ran into trouble with the Inquisition, though we also know of his disappointment with the new king, an absolutist and treacherous monarch, and with the resignation or even indifference of a people who had fought so hard not long before. This disappointment, which was to prompt his distancing from the court, is evident in one of his most sombre works, *The Council of the Philippines* (1816, Musée Goya, Castres).

In 1816 and 1818 he began two further series of prints, *The Art of Bullfighting* and *Absurdities*. In both cases, they were not published during Goya's lifetime but by the Academy in 1864 under the name *Proverbs* in a collection of eighteen prints, and a further four separately. Some of his earlier themes such as the straw manikin, blind man's buff, bulls, monstrous people and gloomy scenes are recognisable. The engravings display greater freedom in the

Self-Portrait with Doctor Arrieta. *The Minneapolis Institute of Arts. Previous double page,* The Third of May 1808: The Mass Execution at Príncipe Pío. *Museo del Prado.*

agradecido, à su amigo Arrieta: por el acierto y esmero con q.^e le salvó la vida en su aguda
y peligrosa enfermedad, padecida à fines del año 1819. a los setenta y tres de su edad. lo pintó en 18

use of the burin and the inking accentuates the sensation of horror of terrifying emotion.

In 1817 Goya received a commission for a new religious painting, this time for the sacristy of Seville cathedral: the large painting of the martyred saints Justa and Rufina, the city's patron saints. The end result was very much in tune with Sevillian taste. The sketch housed at the Prado shows very free brushstrokes and a female model which is out of keeping with devotional taste.

Around this time the artist suffered from a serious illness which added to his deep personal crisis. The moving *Self-Portrait with Doctor Arrieta* (1820, The Minneapolis Institute of Arts) bears witness to his recovery. Goya, sitting up in bed, almost unconscious, is supported by his physician, who helps him drink the medicine that is to save him. Poet Yves Bonnefoy comments that, "Goya has escaped the abysm owing solely to the intervention of Arrieta, who, seated behind him, supporting the back of his neck, his face tense with anxiety, holds out the medicine (...). But is it merely the professional action of the physician that Goya wishes to evoke? (...). We feel the pressure of Arrieta's arm on his friend's shoulder, to prop him up, to bring him nearer to the glass, and we understand that his friend's arm, that last awareness the dying man – who is furthermore deaf – has of the outside world, is the only action that is occurring, the only one that saves him".

The black paintings

In 1819 Goya bought a house outside Madrid, which he called La Quinta del Sordo, and decorated it with fourteen oil paintings done on the walls and framed. They must have been executed while he was recovering from his serious illness between 1820 and 1823, which is when he made the house over to his grandson Mariano. It seems likely that these paintings, which have been studied by historian Nigel Glendinning through photographs and an X-ray examination, were painted over earlier works that adorned the walls and lie beneath what is visible today. The "black paintings", as they were called by the first visitors to the Quinta, defy any rational analysis and are perhaps Goya's means of exorcising and freeing his own nightmares. These totally private works were rarely seen or exhibited before they were transferred to canvas and taken to the Museo del Prado in 1881. They all suffered serious damage during the first restoration carried out by Prado restorer J. J. Arbós.

In the *Duel with Cudgels* (Museo del Prado) Goya reflects upon the violent and absurd death men inflict upon each other, which in this case is the inevitable outcome for one of the two. The same idea of death is developed in the *The Dog* (Museo del Prado) who is doomed to die in the sand.

Other black paintings are *Pilgrimage to the Fountain of St Isidore, The Fates* or *Atropos, The Procession of St Isidore* and *Witches' Sabbath* or *The Great He-Goat* (Museo del Prado) which probably depicts a meeting of witches in which a young girl is initiated in the presence of the devil. In this work it is not the individuals themselves but the overall scene that is important, the idea of a corrupt society which people continue to be tricked into joining. *Saturn Devouring*

Top, Duel with Cudgels. *Bottom,* Witches' Sabbath. *Museo del Prado.*

his Son is directly inspired by a painting by Rubens (Museo del Prado), but whereas Rubens's Saturn is a heroic character, Goya's is a diabolic prince who represents evil from start to finish. The changes made by the restorer are of great iconographic significance as they largely lessen the painting's merit. They relate to Saturn's gaze, which in images dating before the restoration was turned towards the sun, and the censure of Saturn's erect penis, an allusion to the perverse pleasure the god derived from destroying his offspring. *Doña Leocadia Zorrilla* (Museo del Prado), a portrait of his second wife, differs from the other paintings as to theme – it is not a "black painting" as such – and as to the manner in which the subject is depicted, which is more in line with previous portraits of women.

EXILE IN FRANCE (1824-1828)

In 1824 Goya set off for France having been granted royal permission to "take the waters" and be restored to health – a pretext for leaving Spain. Although in principle the repression of Ferdinand VII's reign did not seem to affect Goya, his fears do not appear ungrounded, as his loyalty to the regime was questioned. He made a first stop in Paris and settled in Bordeaux shortly afterwards, probably because his friend Moratín lived there. This was a calm period in Goya's life, even though he at times felt nostalgia for Madrid. *Albums G* and *H* containing pencil sketches of street life or allegorical motifs again show his interest in the world around him. The drawings include a magnificent full-length self-portrait of the artist as a bearded old man; this very expressive image is entitled *I Still Learn*. However, he returned to Madrid on several occasions, on one to settle matters relating to his retirement.

One of his last works, *The Milkmaid of Bordeaux* (Museo del Prado), displays broken colour, and has been considered impressionist owing to the way the brushstrokes are applied. Also around this time he painted a portrait of *Juan Bautista Muguiro* (Museo del Prado), which, despite the artist's ailing eyesight, is a magnificent psychological portrait that is very modern. With a certain amount of pride, Goya added after his signature that he painted it at the age of eighty-one. After the painter's death, it was Muguiro who bought *The Milkmaid of Bordeaux* from Leocadia Weiss.

Goya died in Bordeaux in 1828. His mortal remains currently rest at the chapel of San Antonio de la Florida in Madrid, his burial place since 1919.

Top, Don Juan Bautista Muguiro. *Bottom*, The Milkmaid of Bordeaux. *Museo del Prado.*

© ALDEASA, 2003
I.S.B.N.: 84-8003-383-5
Legal Deposit: M-53572-2003
Photographs:
  © Archivo Museo del Prado
  © The Minneapolis Institute of Arts

Published and produced by: ALDEASA
Written by: Mar Sánchez Ramón
Collection design: A. Ochoa de Zabalegui
Translation: Jenny F. Dodman
Layout: ALDEASA
Photomechanical production: Lucam
Printed by: TF artes gráficas
Front cover illustration: The Clothed Maja *(detail). Museo del Prado*
Back cover illustration: Self-Portrait. *Museo del Prado*